DATE DUE

REVISED AND UPDATED

Kids' Guide to Government

Governments
Around the World

Heinemann Library
Chicago, Illinois

www.heinemannraintree.com
Visit our website to find out more information about Heinemann-Raintree books.

To order:

☎ Phone 888-454-2279

💻 Visit www.heinemannraintree.com to browse our catalog and order online.

Edited by Megan Cotugno
Designed by Ryan Frieson and Tony Miracle
Maps by Mapping Specialists
Picture research by Tracy Cummins and Heather Mauldin
Originated by Dot Gradations
Printed and Bound in the United States by Corporate Graphics

13 12 11 10 09
10 9 8 7 6 5 4 3 2 1

New edition ISBNs: 978-1-4329-2705-9 (hardcover)
                    978-1-4329-2710-3 (paperback)

Library of Congress Cataloging-in-Publication Data

Giesecke, Ernestine, 1945-
    Governments around the world / Ernestine Giesecke.
      p. cm. – (Kids' guide)
    Includes bibliographical references and index.
    Summary: Introduces the concept of government, exploring various types of systems, including democracy, communism, and socialism, and presenting international organizations such as the UN and NATO.
    ISBN 1-57572-511-8 (library binding)
    1. Comparative government—Juvenile literature. [1. Comparative government.] I. Title.
  II. Series.
  JF127.G54 2000
  320.3—dc21

      99-057610

Acknowledgments

The author and publishers are grateful to the following for permission to reproduce copyright material: **p. 4** Associated Press/©Zsolt Szigetvary; **p. 5** Getty Images/©CHRISTOPHE SIMON; **p. 6** Associated Press/©Yaron Kaminsky; **p. 7** NASA/©James B. Irwin; **p. 11** Getty Images/©AFP/GERARD CERLES; **p. 12** Getty Images/©Anwar Hussein Collection; **p. 13** Associated Press/©Buerau of the Royal Household, HO; **p. 14** Getty Images/©AFP/SERGEI SUPINSKY; **p. 15** Associated Press/©AP PHOTO; **p. 16** Alamy/©Pixonnet/Ingemar Edfalk; **p. 17** Alamy/©Paul Gapper; **p. 18** Associated Press/©Jeff Widener; **p. 19** Getty Images/©AFP/LUIS ACOSTA; **p. 20** Shutterstock/©Vishal Shah; **p. 21** Getty Images/©Christian Science Monitor; **p. 22** AP Photo/©The Canadian Press/Tom Hanson; **p. 23** Getty Images/©Hiroyuki Matsumoto; **p. 24** Associated Press/©Frank Franklin II; **p. 25** Alamy/©Reuters/Alan Gignoux; **p. 26** Landov/©Yves Herman; **p. 27** Associated Press/©Pat Roque; **p. 28** Shutterstock/©Ryabitskaya Elena; **p. 29** Getty Images/©AFP/GERARD CERLES

Cover photograph reproduced with permission of Getty Images/©AFP PHOTO/Stan Honda.

We would like to thank Dr. John Allen Williams for his invaluable help in the preparation of this book.

Every effort has been made to contact copyright holders of any material reproduced in this book. Any omissions will be rectified in subsequent printings if notice is given to the publisher.

All the Internet addresses (URLs) given in this book were valid at the time of going to press. However, due to the dynamic nature of the Internet, some addresses may have changed, or sites may have changed or ceased to exist since publication. While the author and Publishers regret any inconvenience this may cause readers, no responsibility for any such changes can be accepted by either the author or the Publishers.

Contents

Some words are shown in bold, **like this**. You can find out what they mean by looking in the glossary.

What Is Government?

A government is the organization of people that directs the actions of a nation, state, or community. A government has the **authority** and power to make, carry out, and **enforce** laws, and to settle disagreements about those laws. Governments have many different structures. Some governments have similar structures, but they act very differently.

The people who lead governments come to power in different ways. Some government leaders are elected, or chosen by the citizens. Other governments are led by people who are related to a previous ruler. Still others are led by people who force their way into power.

Governments may have limited or unlimited power. Power is most often limited by a written **constitution**. In countries with constitutions, both the people and the government know the accepted rules and are supposed to follow them. In some countries, such as Great Britain, the rules are understood and followed even without a written constitution.

> When a group of people have their own government and live within a defined territory, they are known as a nation. There are more than 200 nations in the world today.

When a government has limited power, people can speak out to let the government know what they want.

St. Peter's square is part of Vatican City, in Italy.

Vatican City is a separate nation—the world's smallest—located within the city of Rome, Italy. It is the home of the pope, the leader of the Roman Catholic Church.

In other countries without a constitution, individuals have given themselves unlimited powers. These governments have power over every aspect of people's lives. These governments expect the people to follow strict rules while the government itself follows no rules.

The United States is one of several countries that have a **federal** system. In federalism, governmental power is shared between a central government and divisions of the country, such as states or provinces. Canada, Argentina, and Australia are some other federalist countries.

Most nations have a single central government. Countries such as Sweden and Japan have single governments with a **monarch**. France and the Philippines are single government countries without a monarch.

The Jobs of Government

All governments have some of the same jobs. The most important job is protection. A government must protect itself as well as its people. It should be strong enough to defend against threats from both inside and outside the country.

Many governments also want to protect the rights of individuals. Such governments make laws to prevent people and organizations—even the government itself—from interfering with a person's rights. In some countries, however, the government itself harms people, such as putting them in prison without a trial.

Like other armies, the army in Israel is always alert—ready to protect the nation and its government from outside attack.

One of the jobs of a government is to do things that will bring honor to the nation. The race to put a man on the moon gave the entire United States a goal and helped citizens feel pride in their government.

A government should have a clear and fair way to settle differences among the people it governs. One way most governments do this is through the use of laws and courts.

Another job of a government is to manage the country's resources. These resources are money, the **raw materials** needed to make products, and the people needed to make those products. The government's job is to make sure that people can earn enough money to buy the things they need. This is difficult to do in some countries—either because the resources are scarce or because the government keeps tight control of the resources.

Countries of the World

You will read about many of these countries in this book.

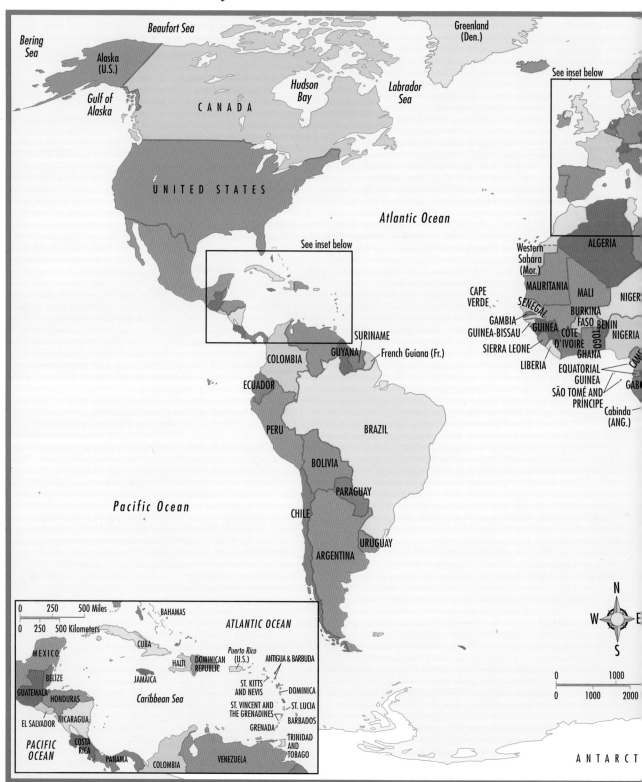

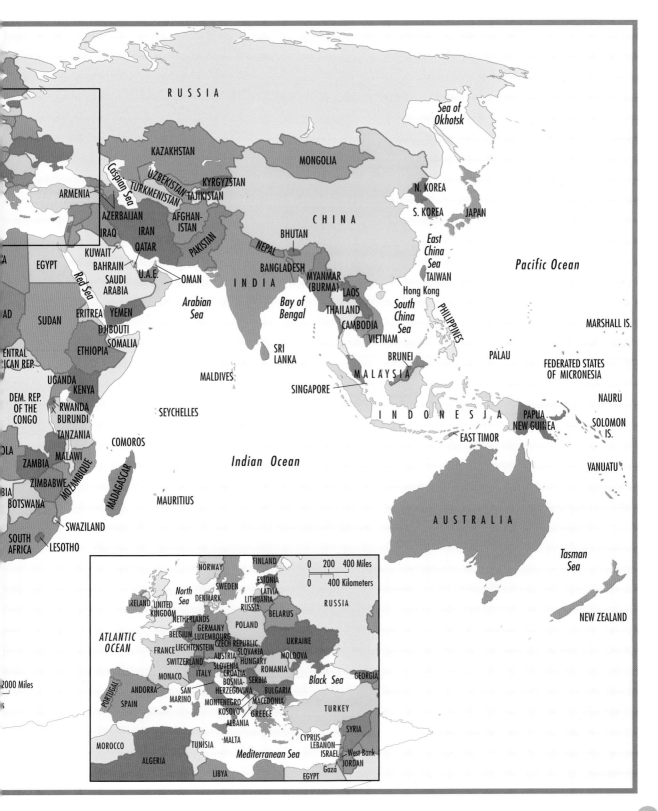

RUSSIA

Sea of
Okhotsk

KAZAKHSTAN

MONGOLIA

Caspian Sea

ARMENIA

UZBEKISTAN
TURKMENISTAN
KYRGYZSTAN
TAJIKISTAN

N. KOREA

S. KOREA   JAPAN

AZERBAIJAN
AFGHAN-
ISTAN

IRAQ

IRAN   QATAR

CHINA

East
China
Sea

Pacific Ocean

KUWAIT
BAHRAIN

PAKISTAN

BHUTAN

NEPAL

TAIWAN

EGYPT

SAUDI
ARABIA

U.A.E.   OMAN

BANGLADESH

INDIA

MYANMAR
(BURMA)

LAOS

Hong Kong

Red Sea

Arabian
Sea

Bay of
Bengal

THAILAND

South
China
Sea

PHILIPPINES

AD

SUDAN   ERITREA   YEMEN

DJIBOUTI

CAMBODIA

VIETNAM

MARSHALL IS.

ENTRAL
ICAN REP.

ETHIOPIA

SOMALIA

SRI
LANKA

MALDIVES

BRUNEI

MALAYSIA

PALAU

FEDERATED STATES
OF MICRONESIA

UGANDA

KENYA

SINGAPORE

NAURU

DEM. REP.
OF THE
CONGO

RWANDA
BURUNDI

INDONESIA

PAPUA
NEW GUINEA

SOLOMON
IS.

SEYCHELLES

TANZANIA

COMOROS

EAST TIMOR

VANUATU

OLA

ZAMBIA

MALAWI

MADAGASCAR

MOZAMBIQUE

Indian Ocean

AUSTRALIA

BIA

ZIMBABWE

MAURITIUS

BOTSWANA

Tasman
Sea

SWAZILAND

SOUTH
AFRICA

LESOTHO

NEW ZEALAND

FINLAND

NORWAY

0   200   400 Miles

0   400 Kilometers

ESTONIA

SWEDEN

North
Sea

LATVIA

DENMARK

LITHUANIA

RUSSIA

IRELAND   UNITED
KINGDOM

RUSSIA

BELARUS

NETHERLANDS

ATLANTIC
OCEAN

GERMANY

POLAND

BELGIUM   LUXEMBOURG

FRANCE   LIECHTENSTEIN

CZECH REPUBLIC
SLOVAKIA

UKRAINE

AUSTRIA

HUNGARY

MOLDOVA

SWITZERLAND

SLOVENIA

CROATIA

ROMANIA

MONACO

ITALY

SERBIA

GEORGIA

2000 Miles

PORTUGAL

ANDORRA

SAN
MARINO

BOSNIA-
HERZEGOVINA

BULGARIA

Black Sea

s

SPAIN

MONTENEGRO

MACEDONIA

KOSOVO

GREECE

TURKEY

ALBANIA

MALTA

SYRIA

MOROCCO

TUNISIA

Mediterranean Sea

CYPRUS

LEBANON

ISRAEL   West Bank

ALGERIA

LIBYA

EGYPT

Gaza   JORDAN

Constitutional Governments

A **constitution** is a document that describes the authority and power of a government. It tells what powers the government has and describes the limits of those powers.

A constitution usually describes how power is passed from one person to another. It tells when and how people can be elected, as well as who is qualified to be elected. And, it might tell how long a person can remain in power.

Many nations with written constitutions are **democracies** or **republics**. In such nations, the people elect, or choose, their leaders. The United States is a democracy. Here, the authority and power for making, **enforcing**, and explaining laws is shared among three branches of government. There is a **chief executive**, a **legislature**, and a top, or supreme, court. Each has a special job to do. No one person or branch can get too much power.

> The United States Constitution, approved by nine states in 1787, is the world's oldest written constitution.

A constitution
• describes the government
• lists the purposes of the government
• describes the rights of the people
• defines and limits the powers of the leaders
• tells how leaders are elected and how long they can stay in office.

Like presidents in other countries with constitutional governments, the French president, Nicolas Sarkozy, reports to the legislature on the country's well-being.

France is a republic. Its president, the **chief of state**, is elected. The head of government is the prime minister, appointed by the president. Members of the legislature (the National Assembly) are elected. France has a **free-market economy**, but the government owns railway, electricity, aircraft, and telephone companies.

The United States of America is a **federal** republic. The head of government, the president, is elected by the people. Members of the legislature are also elected by the people.

Some countries have constitutions that are written by or changed by a few powerful people. These constitutions are more like statements telling who is in charge, and they do not describe any limits to the government's power. This may result in unlimited, **authoritarian**, or even **totalitarian** governments.

Monarchies

A monarchy is a government led by a single permanent ruler, usually a king or a queen. This ruler, called a **monarch**, often gains power from his or her parents or another relative.

There are not many true monarchies left in the world today. However, monarchs rule several countries in North Africa and the Middle East, often with the king as an **absolute ruler.** This may result in an **authoritarian**—or even **totalitarian**—government.

The United Kingdom (sometimes called Great Britain) is a constitutional monarchy, but its government is more like a democracy. It has both a monarch and a **constitution.** The constitution is not a written constitution. Instead, it consists of many laws passed over the centuries.

The **legislature** has two houses: the House of Lords and the House of Commons. There is a prime minister, who is the head of the government. The leader of the **political party** with the most seats in the house of commons becomes the prime minister.

In a constitutional monarchy, the duties of the monarch are mostly ceremonial. Here, Queen Elizabeth of Great Britain addresses the parliament.

This procession honors His Majesty King Bhumibol Adulyadej, who has served as Thailand's monarch for over 60 years and is the world's longest reigning monarch.

Some countries have both a monarch and a constitution. In these countries, the king or queen acts as the head of state. He or she represents the country to the rest of the world. The monarch of a constitutional monarchy plays an important role in national events but usually does not have great **political** power. The country is actually ruled by people who are elected according to the constitution.

There are few absolute monarchies left on earth. Saudi Arabia was an absolute monarchy until 1992. Since then, the king has been elected, but only by members of his royal family.

Dictatorships

Sometimes the government of a country just doesn't work well. Perhaps most of the people are poor and hungry, and people working in government use their positions to take money for doing favors. These things make the government weak.

When a government is weak, other people may try to take it over. Often, members of the **military overthrow** the government. This is because military forces have both the weapons and the power to do so.

Libya is a military dictatorship. Muammar al-Qaddafi overthrew a monarchy in 1969 and took over as **chief of state**. He rewrote the **constitution** and established a legislature called the General People's Congress. It is run by a single **political party**—his own.

Muammar al-Qaddafi is the military dictator of Libya. He has been in power since 1969.

Idi Amin speaks at a rally on January 25, 1978, celebrating the seventh anniversary of his rule as president of Uganda.

Once the military has taken over the government, the new leaders may begin to make changes. They might decide that the constitution, if one existed, should be put aside for a while. The military leader becomes a dictator—an **absolute ruler**. He or she may establish his or her own rules and ignore the laws of the country.

A dictatorship is often a **totalitarian** government. Because dictators do not want the people to know the truth about what is happening, they usually take control of media such as television stations and newspapers. They may also prevent people from gathering in groups to protest the new government. Dictators usually severely punish people who disagree with them.

The African country of Uganda was under the rule of dictator Idi Amin from 1971–1979. When he first came to power, many Ugandans thought he would bring about change and prosperity to their country. However, Amin's rule soon turned into one of fear and terror, as word spread that he was murdering his people. He was eventually forced to flee Uganda and lived in exile until his death in 2003.

Socialism

A government can also be described by the way it manages a nation's **economic** resources. A country's resources include natural resources, such as iron ore to make steel and good soil to grow food. It also includes human resources, such as workers who mine the iron ore, turn it into steel, and then form it into tractors. It could also include farmers who plant crops, harvest them, and bring them to market.

Socialism is one way governments can manage a country's resources. One of the goals of a **socialist** government is to give all citizens an equal share in the products and services of the country. Generally, a socialist government tries to achieve this equality by creating and then following an economic plan that affects all parts of society.

Sweden's economy is a combination of **free-market** and socialism. Most of the country's economy is privately owned, but the country has a **welfare** system that gives all citizens **benefits**, such as health care and retirement income.

Income taxes in Sweden are among the highest in the world because the government provides free health care and child care to its citizens.

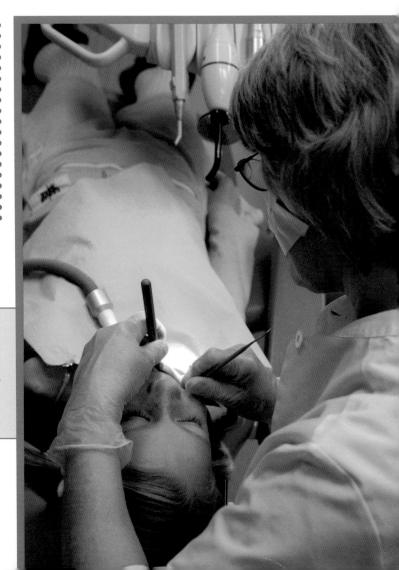

The government of Norway owns and runs nearly all of the railroads in the country.

In many socialist countries, the government controls all large businesses that affect everyone, such as railroads, airlines, and telephones. In some cases, the government itself owns and manages the businesses. In other cases, the businesses are owned by individuals, but are under the government's tight control.

A socialist government requires people who work to give a large part of what they make to the government, usually as income tax. The government uses this money to provide benefits for all the people. This way, even citizens who can't work can still have a good life. Many socialist governments offer all citizens free health care, free education, affordable housing, and a comfortable retirement income.

Norway is a constitutional monarchy with a king as **chief of state**. The head of government, the **prime minister**, is appointed by the king and approved by the **legislature**.

Communism

Communism is another way a government can manage the country's resources. Under this system of government, the people own all the resources, including farms, factories, and stores.

In a **communist** country, the leaders of the Communist Party make important government decisions. They decide the **economic** plan and how it will be carried out. There may be an elected **legislature**, but it usually has little power. Programs proposed by the Communist Party leaders are automatically approved.

Cuba is a communist nation. The government controls all farming, industry, and foreign trade. The **chief of state** and head of government for over 50 years was Fidel Castro, whose army captured power in 1959. Castro's brother Raul became chief of state and head of government in 2008. There is an elected legislature, but there is only one **political party**.

When students in the People's Republic of China spoke out against government policy, the government sent the army to silence them.

Cuban cigar makers work rolling cigars at a factory in Havana, Cuba.

The government plans what resources will be used and who will use them. It also plans what products will be made and who will make them. Finally, the government decides how the finished products, as well as the **profits** from them, will be divided among the people.

People in communist countries are often told what kind of work they can do. They are told whether they can become a college professor or a factory worker. Both college professors and factory workers are paid by the government, and may earn about the same amount.

Countries with a communist economic system usually have an **authoritarian** or **totalitarian** government. Only the communist political party is recognized, and disagreement with the government is not allowed.

Capitalism

Some governments choose not to be involved in the production of goods or in the creation of services. Instead, they help privately owned businesses grow and prosper. This situation is called a **free-market economy,** or **capitalism**.

Singapore has a free-market economy. The country and its people profit from their work. Singapore is a **republic** within a group of countries called a commonwealth. The president is the **chief of state** and is elected by **popular vote**. Members of the **legislature** are also elected by popular vote. However, there is only one major **political party,** which makes the government somewhat **authoritarian**.

Singapore does not have many natural resources, but it does have a large labor force. Singapore specializes in manufacturing labor-intensive items.

In a free-market economy, this violin craftsman is able to make and sell as many, or as few, items as he wishes.

Japan has a free-market economy. It is also a constitutional monarchy. There are two legislative houses, whose members are elected. There are many political parties.

In nations with free markets, the people and the government work together to make a **profit**. People who supply **raw materials**, make products, and sell the products all work together. In a free-market economy, the government often allows individuals and companies to sell their products and services for as much as other people or companies are willing to pay.

Empires and Commonwealths

There are no true empires in the world today. An empire was a group of different countries held together by military force. The people in the countries in an empire had different ways of living, different backgrounds, and different languages, but they were ruled by the strongest country in the group.

Britain once had one of the largest empires in the world. For three hundred years, from the mid-1600s to the mid-1900s, the British Empire included places as far apart as Canada and Australia and as different as Hong Kong and South Africa. Britain created the empire primarily to get the **raw materials** to make new products and to create new places to sell those products.

Canada is a member of the Commonwealth of Nations. Canada's government is a **democracy**. Its **chief of state** is the British monarch, who is represented in Canada by a governor. Queen Elizabeth II of Britain chooses the governor with the advice of Canada's **prime minister**, who is the head of the country's government and the leader of the major **political party**. Canada has a **free-market economy**.

Prime Minister Stephen Harper of Canada addresses supporters, workers, and members of the Federal Conservative Caucus.

The Great Barrier Reef of Australia was once part of the British Empire. Today, Australia and other countries are part of the Commonwealth of Nations.

A commonwealth is a group of countries that forms for the good (the "common wealth") of all its member countries. The largest commonwealth is the Commonwealth of Nations, formed of more than 50 nations that were once part of the British Empire. The leaders of Commonwealth nations meet to discuss matters of importance to all the countries and to work toward common **economic** goals.

The Commonwealth of Independent States is made up of 12 nations that were formerly part of the **Soviet Union**. This commonwealth was formed to help keep the peace between countries that had been under tight **communist** rule.

The United Nations

At different times in history, countries have chosen to work together. Sometimes, several nations joined forces against a country that had more wealth or power.

At the end of **World War II**, some nations decided to work together in order to avoid war in the future. These nations formed the United Nations, or UN. The United Nations is not a government. Although it does not make laws, many believe the UN does have the force of law. It has no army. Instead, the United Nations provides a way for governments to work out their differences.

> The UN Charter lists four purposes: "to maintain international peace and security, to develop friendly relations among nations, to cooperate in solving international problems and in promoting respect for human rights, and to be a center for harmonizing the actions of nations."

Everything that is said during a meeting of the UN is translated into many languages, so that everyone will understand.

The UN has sent food and medical supplies throughout the world to help countries improve the health and living conditions of their people.

The United Nations was founded in 1945 by 51 nations, including the United States. Today, 192 nations belong to the UN. The main offices of the United Nations are in New York City. There are other UN offices in Geneva, Switzerland; Nairobi, Kenya; and Vienna, Austria.

The countries that started the United Nations in 1945 wrote a statement, called the UN Charter, describing their plans. Member countries promise to live together in peace and to work together to keep the rest of the world peaceful without having to use force. They voluntarily supply peacekeeping forces made up of soldiers who can be sent to areas where local **conflict** threatens peace.

Countries that belong to the United Nations also work together to improve the health and living conditions of people around the world. They help people recover and rebuild from disasters such as floods and earthquakes.

Other International Organizations

In today's world, there are many different groups of nations that work together for various purposes. Some are alliances, which are groups of countries pledged to support one another in times of **conflict**. Others work together to improve trade among the members.

Like the United Nations, these organizations are not a form of government. They do not make laws or have armies. Rather, they offer governments a way to work together. One nation can belong to many different groups.

There were 28 members of NATO in 2009: Albania, Belgium, Bulgaria, Canada, Croatia, Czech Republic, Denmark, Estonia, France, Germany, Greece, Hungary, Iceland, Italy, Latvia, Lithuania, Luxembourg, Netherlands, Norway, Poland, Portugal, Romania, Slovakia, Slovenia, Spain, Turkey, the United Kingdom, and the U.S.

Like the United Nations, NATO has the ability to send peacekeeping forces from member nations to places where there is conflict.

ASEAN members work together, so their economic strength grows.

One of the oldest organizations is the North Atlantic Treaty Organization (NATO). NATO was formed after **World War II.** Twelve countries, including the United States, promised to come to one another's aid in case of another war or conflict. Over time, the organization has changed. Twenty-eight NATO countries now work together to try and bring about peace without having to use force.

The Association of Southeast Asian Nations (ASEAN) was formed in 1967 to help the economies of countries in Southeast Asia grow. These countries realized that when their governments worked together, they could create more wealth than if each country worked alone.

ASEAN members in 2009 included Brunei, Cambodia, Indonesia, Laos, Malaysia, Myanmar (Burma), the Philippines, Singapore, Thailand, and Vietnam.

The European Union

If you take a five-hour train trip in the United States, you may go through one or more states. But you will still be in the same country, able to spend the same money. Almost everyone you meet will speak the same language.

In Europe, on the other hand, a five-hour train trip will take you through at least two, maybe even three, different countries. Each country has its own money and language.

Some European nations began to work together about 50 years ago to rebuild their countries after **World War II.** They discovered that if they worked with their neighbor nations, they would be able to rebuild faster, and it was less likely they would go to war against one another again.

In many European Union countries, local currency has been replaced by a currency called the Euro.

The European Union began as an economic organization, but today it deals with issues that range from law enforcement to politics.

They founded a simple organization called the European **Economic** Union (known as the Common Market). This organization broke down barriers that made it difficult to **trade** with so many different countries. Today, this simple idea has turned into the European Union, or EU, which now has 27 member nations and a **legislature**—the European **Parliament**. Countries that join the European Union do not have to give up their constitutions or change their governments. They do not have give up their own languages.

The main purpose of the EU is to bring the people in the separate countries of Europe closer together. It is now easier for people to travel from one country to another and for each country to buy from or sell to each other. The EU has also developed a **currency** called the Euro that will replace the many different currencies used by most member countries.

In 2009 there were 27 members of the EU. Members included countries such as Austria, France, Germany, Greece, Ireland, Italy, Luxembourg, the Netherlands, Portugal, Spain, Sweden, and the United Kingdom. The number is likely to increase in coming years.

Glossary

absolute ruler ruler with the power to make all the laws, enforce all the laws, and decide the punishment for breaking the laws; ruler with unlimited power

authority power to enforce laws, command obedience, or judge

authoritarian power is in the hands of one or a few individuals

benefit something provided by a government to its citizens, such as health care, education, housing, or retirement income

capitalism economic system in which individuals may own natural resources, factories, and products, and may keep the money they make from selling them

chief executive top person in the executive branch

chief of state person who is the head of a national government

communist economic system in which natural resources, land, factories, and products are owned by all people in the community, and all citizens share the money that is made from selling them

confederation group of provinces or territories that band together

conflict situation in which groups of people or countries strongly disagree with one another and may possibly fight

constitution written document describing the basic laws or principles by which a government is organized; a description of power and its limits

currency money used in a country

democracy rule by the majority of the people who are governed

economic having to do with the the way that a country manages its money and the products it makes and uses

enforce to make people obey

federal referring to a group of states that give up some power to a central government

free-market economy system of trade that permits individuals to make and sell as many items as they like

hereditary passed on by parents or ancestors

income tax money paid to a government based on the amount of money a person earns

interfere to get in the way of

legislature group of people with power to make and change a nation's laws, also called a parliament

military armed forces such as the army, marines, or air force

monarch ruler such as a king or queen

overthrow to bring down or cause to fall apart, often by use of force

parliament group of people with power to make and change a nation's laws, also called a legislature

political having to do with government

political party group of people who have similar views about government

popular vote election in which ordinary citizens make their choices known

prime minister high government official often appointed by a ruler or chosen by the political party with the most members in the legislature

profit money earned when an item is sold for more than it cost to make

province political unit of a nation or empire; similar to a state

raw material something that can be made into another product after being processed in some way

republic government in which the citizens hold the power and elect individuals to serve as leaders and representatives

socialist relating to the belief that a government should own the means of producing goods so that no one is poor

Soviet Union communist country that included Russia and other nations, and that was divided into separate countries in 1991

trade business of buying and selling goods

totalitarian relating to a government that attempts to control every part of a person's life

welfare providing funds for health care and a minimum standard of living for those who can't afford these things

World War II war involving Great Britain, France, the Soviet Union, and the United States against Germany, Italy, and Japan—as well as the allies of these nations—fought in Europe, Asia, and Africa from 1939 to 1945

Find Out More

Books

Downing, David. *Dictatorship* (*Political and Economic Systems*). Chicago: Heinemann Library, 2008.

Woolf, Alex. *Systems of Government: Democracy*. Strongsville, OH: Gareth Stevens, 2006.

Websites

http://www.nato.int/
Learn more about the North Atlantic Treaty Organization (NATO) and its member countries at this informative site.

http://www.aseansec.org/
This is the official site of ASEAN and its member countries. Learn the history of this organization, as well as contact information.

http://www.un.org/Pubs/CyberSchoolBus/
This site, sponsored by the United Nations, is designed specifically for students. You can educate yourself about world hunger, poverty, and other issues affecting the globe.

Index